About
Skill Builders
Spanish
Level 1
by Ellen Parrish

Welcome to RBP Books' Skill Builders series. Like our Summer Bridge Activities collection, the Skill Builders series is designed to make learning fun and rewarding.

Skill Builders Spanish Level 1 introduces beginning Spanish students to the alphabet, numbers, shapes, colors, and names for parts of the body in Spanish. Activities are designed to give plenty of practice and review to help reinforce new vocabulary at an easy pace. This makes language acquisition less intimidating as students read, write, draw, color, and match their way to better proficiency.

Learning is more effective when approached with an element of fun and enthusiasm. That's why the Skill Builders combine academically sound exercises with engaging graphics and entertaining themes—to make reviewing basic skills at school or home fun and effective, for both you and your budding scholars.

Table of Contents

Los números—Numbers

Practice writing the numbers one to five in Spanish on the lines below.

1	uno	one
2	dos	two
3	tres	three
4	cuatro	four
5	cinco	five

1._____

2._____

3._____

4._____

5._____

Los números—Numbers

Practice writing the numbers six to ten in Spanish on the lines below.

6	seis	six
7	siete	seven
8	ocho	eight
9	nueve	nine
10	diez	ten

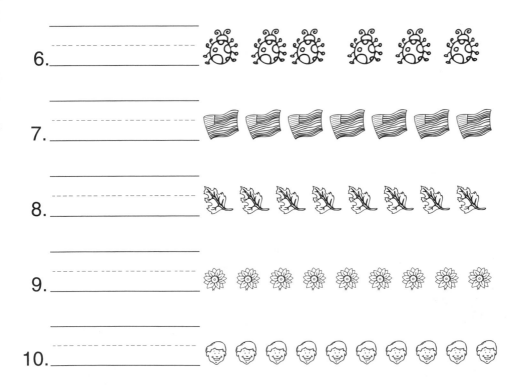

6.

7.

8.

9.

10.

Emparejemos—Matching

Draw a line to match the numbers.

seven	ocho	3
three	tres	8
eight	diez	10
two	siete	2
ten	dos	7
one	nueve	9
four	uno	1
nine	cuatro	6
five	seis	4
six	cinco	5

Spanish Level 1—RBP0148

Los números—Numbers

Write the Spanish number and draw the correct number of circles in each box as shown.

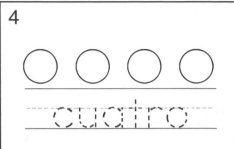

5	10

1	7

3	6

¿Cuántos son?—How many?

Write the correct number in each box as shown.

Los números—Numbers

Color the correct number of rectangles.

dos	▨	▨								
nueve										
cuatro										
uno										
ocho										
siete										
tres										
cinco										
diez										
seis										

¡Bien!
(Good!)

El alfabeto—The Alphabet

The Spanish alphabet has 29 letters. Write the underlined letter in each Spanish word and color the pictures below. Write each letter in lower- and uppercase. The first one is done for you.

<u>a</u>vión—airplane

<u>b</u>allena—whale

<u>c</u>onejo—rabbit

<u>ch</u>aqueta—jacket

<u>d</u>inero—money

 Say the names of the letters: *a* = ah, *b* = beh, *c* = seh, *ch* = cheh, *d* = deh.

El alfabeto—The Alphabet

Write the underlined letter in each Spanish word and color
the pictures below. Write each letter in lower- and uppercase.

elefante—elephant

flor—flower

gallo—rooster

hoja—leaf

isla—island

Say the names of the letters: e = eh, f = eh-feh, g = heh,
h = ah-cheh (note: the "h" is silent in Spanish), i = ee.

El alfabeto—The Alphabet

Write the underlined letter in each Spanish word and color the pictures below. Write each letter in lower- and uppercase.

juguete—toy	kilómetro—kilometer
libro—book	lluvia—rain
manzana—apple	nube—cloud

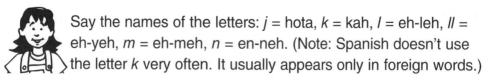

Say the names of the letters: *j* = hota, *k* = kah, *l* = eh-leh, *ll* = eh-yeh, *m* = eh-meh, *n* = en-neh. (Note: Spanish doesn't use the letter *k* very often. It usually appears only in foreign words.)

El alfabeto—The Alphabet

Write the underlined letter in each Spanish word and color
the pictures below. Write each letter in lower- and uppercase.

niño—boy

oso—bear

pato—duck

queso—cheese

regalo—gift

Say the names of the letters: ñ = en-yeh, o = oh, p = pe,
q = coo, r = eh-ray. (Note: the r in Spanish is pronounced
with a trill, or what is sometimes called a "rolled" r.)

El alfabeto—The Alphabet

Write the underlined letter in each Spanish word and color
the pictures below. Write each letter in lower- and uppercase.

pe__rr__o—dog

The sol (sun) is so hot today!

__s__ol—sun

__t__ambor—drum

__u__no—one

__v__aca—cow

Say the names of the letters: *s* = eh-seh, *t* = teh, *u* = oo, *v* = beh. *Rr* (eh-rreh) is not found at the beginning or any Spanish words, but it does have its own sound. Practice rolling the *rr* with your tongue on the roof of your mouth: r-r-r-r-r-r.

El alfabeto—The Alphabet

Write the underlined letter in each Spanish word and color the pictures below. Write each letter in lower- and uppercase.

Uno, dos, buckle my zapato (shoe).

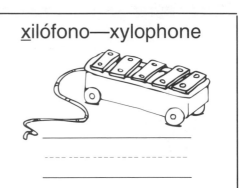

x̲ilófono—xylophone

_____

- - - - - - - - - - - - - -

W

_____

- - - - - - - - - - - - - -

y̲erba—herb

_____

- - - - - - - - - - - - - -

What about *w*? In Spanish, *w* and *k* usually only appear in words that come from another language. But you can color the letter so it doesn't feel left out.

z̲apato—shoe

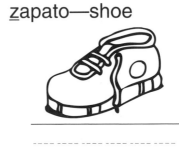

_____

- - - - - - - - - - - - - -

Say the names of the letters: *w* = doble-beh, *x* = eh-kis, *y* = ee-griega, *z* = seh-tah.

Pronunciación—Pronunciation

Color the Spanish vowels.

 Spanish vowels are very simple to pronounce. There is only one sound for each vowel: *a* = ah, *e* = eh, *i* = ee, *o* = oh, *u* = oo, and *y* = ee.

Repasemos—Let's Review the Alphabet

Practice writing these words that begin with *a*.

A _____   a _____

agua

alto

abril

ángel

árbol

Repasemos—Let's Review the Alphabet

Practice writing these words that begin with *b*.

B _____   b _____

balón _____

boca _____

bebé _____

brazo _____

búho _____

Which words do you recognize from the list?
Key: balón—ball   boca—mouth   bebé—baby
        brazo—arm   búho—owl

15

Repasemos—Let's Review the Alphabet

Practice writing these words that begin with *c*.

C _____   c _____

casa

cara

caja

cola

cien 100

Which words do you recognize from the list?

Key: casa—house   cara—face   caja—box
          cola—tail   cien—100

Repasemos—Let's Review the Alphabet

Practice writing these words that begin with *ch*.

Ch _____   ch _____

chal

chiste

chaqueta

chicle

chocolate

 Which words do you recognize from the list?
Key: chal—shawl   chiste—joke   chaqueta—jacket
          chicle—gum   chocolate—chocolate

Repasemos—Let's Review the Alphabet

Practice writing these words that begin with *d*.

D _____   d _____

duro

dama

diez

diente

dedo

Which words do you recognize from the list?

Key: duro—hard   dama—lady   diez—ten
        diente—tooth   dedo—finger

Repasemos—Let's Review the Alphabet

Practice writing these words that begin with e.

E _____   e _____

elfo

escuela

éxito

eso

estómago

Which words do you recognize from the list?
Key: elfo—elf   escuela—school   éxito—success
      eso—that   estómago—stomach

Repasemos—Let's Review the Alphabet

Practice writing these words that begin with *f*.

F _____   f _____

flor

feliz

foca

fresa

fútbol

 Which words do you recognize from the list?

Key: flor—flower   feliz—happy   foca—seal
         fresa—strawberry   fútbol—soccer

Repasemos—Let's Review the Alphabet

Practice writing these words that begin with _g_.

G _____   g _____

gallo

gorra

granja

gato

gusano

Which words do you recognize from the list?
Key: gallo—rooster   gorra—cap   granja—farm
        gato—cat   gusano—worm

Spanish Level 1—RBP0148

Repasemos—Let's Review the Alphabet

Practice writing these words that begin with *h*.

H _____   h _____

hielo

hermana

horno

hormiga

hola   Hello!

Which words do you recognize from the list?
Key: hielo—ice   hermana—sister   horno—oven
        hormiga—ant   hola—hello

Repasemos—Let's Review the Alphabet

Practice writing these words that begin with *i*.

I _____   i _____

iguana

isla

idea

inglés   English

¡Bien!
(Good!)

Which words do you recognize from the list?
Key: iguana—iguana   isla—island
              idea—idea   inglés—English

Repasemos—Let's Review the Alphabet

Practice writing these words that begin with _j_.

J _____   j _____

jugo

jardín

joya

jugar

Which words do you recognize from the list?
Key: jugo—juice   jardín—garden
          joya—jewel   jugar—to play

Repasemos—Let's Review the Alphabet

Practice writing these words that begin with *k* and *l*.

K _____   k _____

L _____   l _____

kilómetro _____

león _____

luna _____

libro _____

limón _____

 Which words do you recognize from the list?

Key: kilómetro—kilometer   león—lion   luna—moon
       libro—book   limón—lemon

                           Spanish Level 1—RBP0148

Repasemos—Let's Review the Alphabet

Practice writing these words that begin with *ll*.

LL _____   ll _____

llama

lluvia

llanta

llave

llorar

 Which words do you recognize from the list?

Key: llama—llama   lluvia—rain   llanta—tire
        llave—key   llorar—to cry

Repasemos—Let's Review the Alphabet

Practice writing these words that begin with *m*.

M _____   m _____

mano

mundo

mar

mono

maestra

Which words do you recognize from the list?
Key: mano—hand   mundo—world   mar—sea
       mono—monkey   maestra—female teacher

Repasemos—Let's Review the Alphabet

Practice writing these words that use *n* or *ñ*.

N _____   n _____

nuez

nido

nube

niño

nieve

Which words do you recognize from the list?
Key: nuez—nut   nido—nest   nube—cloud
        niño—boy   nieve—snow

Repasemos—Let's Review the Alphabet

Practice writing these words that begin with _o_.

O _____ o _____

oso

oreja

onda

ojo

orca

Which words do you recognize from the list?

Key: oso—bear   oreja—ear   onda—wave
       ojo—eye   orca—killer whale

Repasemos—Let's Review the Alphabet

Practice writing these words that begin with _p_.

P _____   p _____

pato

pan

pollo

pluma

pie

Which words do you recognize from the list?
Key: pato—duck   pan—bread   pollo—chicken
              pluma—pen   pie—foot

Repasemos—Let's Review the Alphabet

Practice writing these words that begin with *q* and *r*.

Q _____ q _____

R _____ r _____

queso

quince

rey

reloj

regalo

 Which words do you recognize from the list?
Key: queso—cheese   quince—fifteen   rey—king
reloj—clock   regalo—gift

Repasemos—Let's Review the Alphabet

Practice writing these words that begin with *s*.

S _____   s _____

sol

silla

sí

sal

siete

 Which words do you recognize from the list?
Key: sol—sun   silla—chair   sí—yes
         sal—salt   siete—seven

Repasemos—Let's Review the Alphabet

Practice writing these words that begin with *t*.

T _____   t _____

tigre

trompa

tres

tren

tambor

Which words do you recognize from the list?
Key: tigre—tiger   trompa—horn   tres—three
          tren—train   tambor—drum

Repasemos—Let's Review the Alphabet

Practice writing these words that begin with *u* and *v*.

U _____   u _____

V _____   v _____

uvas

uno

vaca

vaso

violín

Which words do you recognize from the list?
Key: uno—one   uvas—grapes   vaca—cow
        vaso—vase   violín—violin

Repasemos—Let's Review the Alphabet

Practice writing these words that begin with *x*, *y*, and *z*.

X _____   x _____

Y _____   y _____

Z _____   z _____

xilófono _____

yema _____

zorro _____

zapato _____

Which words do you recognize from the list?
Key: xilófono—xylophone   yema—yolk
            zorro—fox   zapato—shoe

Practiquemos más los números— More Number Practice

In Spanish, write out the numbers backwards from ten to one.

10. _____

9. _____

8. _____

7. _____

6. _____

5. _____

4. _____

3. _____

2. _____

1. _____

Más números en Español— More Spanish Numbers

In Spanish, write out the numbers 11–20 in the spaces provided. Do your best work.

once   once

doce

trece

catorce

quince

dieciséis

diecisiete

dieciocho

diecinueve

veinte

Emparejemos—Matching

Draw a line to match the numbers.

seventeen	dieciocho	13
thirteen	trece	18
eighteen	veinte	20
twelve	diecisiete	12
twenty	doce	17
eleven	diecinueve	19
fourteen	once	11
nineteen	catorce	16
fifteen	dieciséis	14
sixteen	quince	15

¿Cuántos son?—How many?

Count the pictures; then write the correct number in each box as shown.

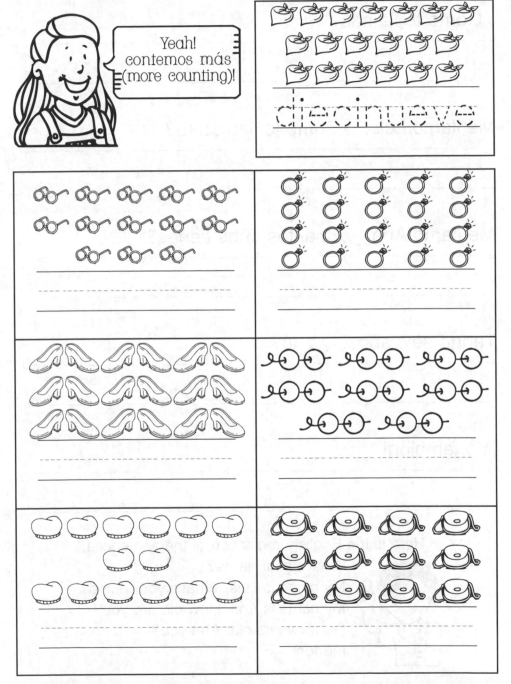

Yeah! contemos más (more counting)!

diecinueve

Practiquemos la escritura—
Let's Practice Writing

Copy the following sentences:

¿Cómo te llamas?

_____

- -

_____

Me llamo Luis. ¿Cómo te llamas tú?

_____

- -

_____

Me llamo Ana. ¿Cuántos años tienes?

_____

- -

_____

Tengo seis años. ¿Y tú?

_____

- -

_____

¡Yo también!

_____

- -

_____

Here is the English translation of the sentences.
What's your name?
My name is Luis. What's your name?
My name is Ana. How old are you?
I'm six years old. And you?
Me too!

Los colores—Colors

Let's learn the names of the colors in Spanish. Color the pictures.

red	rojo	
orange	anaranjado	
yellow	amarillo	
green	verde	

Say the names of the colors.

red	rojo	(row-ho)
orange	anaranjado	(ah-nah-rahn-ha-thoh)
yellow	amarillo	(ah-mah-ree-yo)
green	verde	(behr-theh)

Los colores—Colors

Let's learn the names of the colors in Spanish. Color the pictures.

blue	azul	
purple	morado	
white	blanco	
black	negro	

Say the names of the colors.

blue	azul	(ah-zsool)
purple	morado	(mo-rah-thoh)
white	blanco	(blahn-coh)
black	negro	(neh-grow)

Los colores—Colors

Let's learn the names of the colors in Spanish. Color the pictures.

brown	café	![log]
pink	rosa	![rose]
gray	gris	![cloud]
violet	violeta	![flower]

Say the names of the colors.

brown	café	(cah-feh)
pink	rosa	(row-suh)
gray	gris	(grees)
violet	violeta	(bee-oh-let-uh)

Spanish Level 1—RBP0148

Un arco iris—A Rainbow

Create the colors of a rainbow. Color each bar with the correct color.

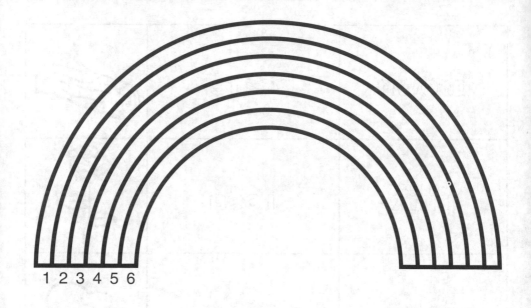

1 2 3 4 5 6

1. rojo

2. anaranjado

3. amarillo

4. verde

5. azul

6. morado

Word Bank

red—rojo

orange—anaranjado

yellow—amarillo

green—verde

blue—azul

purple—morado

Los colores—Colors

Practice writing the names of colors in Spanish.

negro

negro

blanco

amarillo

café

rojo

azul

Los colores—Colors

Practice writing the names of colors in Spanish.

anaranjado

anaranjado

morado

verde

violeta

rosa

gris

Emparejemos—Matching

Connect the name of the color with its picture as shown. Then color the pictures.

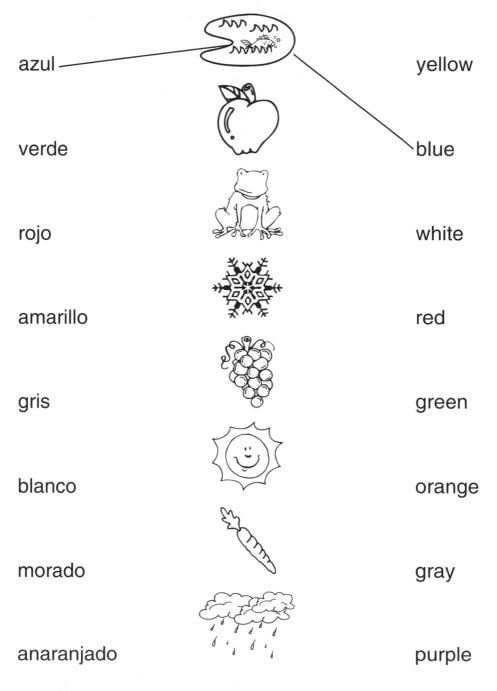

azul

verde

rojo

amarillo

gris

blanco

morado

anaranjado

yellow

blue

white

red

green

orange

gray

purple

El color azul—Blue

Color the pictures below blue. Then, write out the words.

agua	pez
_____	_____
coche	lago
_____	_____
ojo	río
_____	_____

El color rojo—Red

Color the pictures below red. Then, write out the words.

fresa	rosa
manzana	corazón
labios	señal

El color amarillo—Yellow

Color the pictures below yellow. Then, write out the words.

lápiz	sol
plátano	luna
limón	luz

El color anaranjado—Orange

Color the pictures below orange. Then, write out the words.

melón	planeta
_____	_____
calabaza	naranja
_____	_____
fuego	zorro
_____	_____

El color verde—Green

Color the pictures below green. Then, write out the words.

rana		pluma	
hoja		pino	
árbol		aguacate	

El color morado—Purple

Color the pictures below purple. Then, write out the words.

uvas	silla
pelota	jugo
regalo	camiseta

El color negro—Black

Color the pictures below black. Then, write out the words.

araña	llanta
nota	hormiga
gato	teléfono

El color café—Brown

Color the pictures below blue. Then, write out the words.

oso	bate
_____	_____
- - - - - - - - - -	- - - - - - - - - -
_____	_____
pastel	chocolate
_____	_____
- - - - - - - - - -	- - - - - - - - - -
_____	_____
perro	vaca
_____	_____
- - - - - - - - - -	- - - - - - - - - -
_____	_____

El color rosa—Pink

Color the pictures below pink. Then, write out the words.

lengua	mariposa
flor	helado
zapatos	bolsa

El color gris—Gray

Color the pictures below gray. Then, write out the words.

lobo	rata
elefante	botas
mono	nube

Aprendamos las formas—
Let's Learn Shapes

**Practice writing the Spanish words for these shapes.
Color the shapes.**

triángulo

cuadrado

círculo

rectángulo

Pronounce the shapes aloud.

triangle	triángulo	(tree-ahn-goo-low)
square	cuadrado	(kwah-drah-thoh)
circle	círculo	(seer-koo-low)
rectangle	rectángulo	(rec-tahn-goo-low)

Aprendamos las formas—
Let's Learn Shapes

Practice writing the Spanish words for these shapes.
Color the shapes.

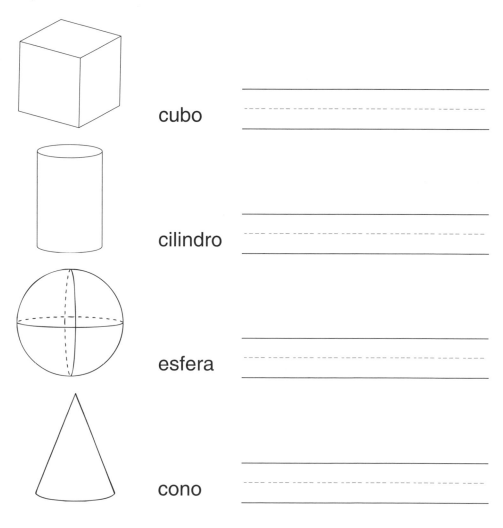

cubo

cilindro

esfera

cono

Pronounce the shapes aloud.

cube	cubo	(koo-boh)
cylinder	cilindro	(see-leen-droh)
sphere	esfera	(es-fair-uh)
cone	cono	(koh-no)

Aprendamos las formas—
Let's Learn Shapes

Practice writing the Spanish words for these shapes.
Color the shapes.

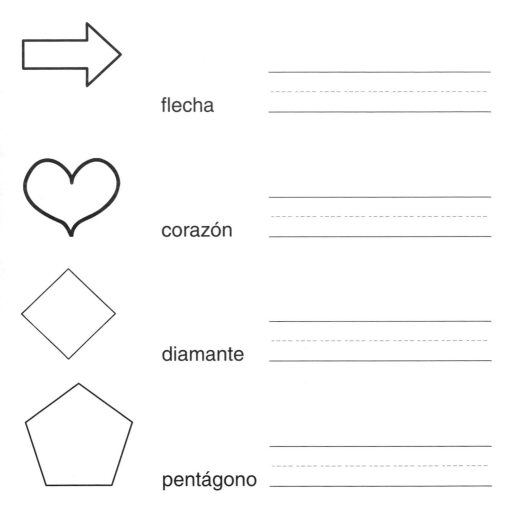

flecha _____

corazón _____

diamante _____

pentágono _____

Pronounce the shapes aloud.

arrow	flecha	(fleh-chuh)
heart	corazón	(ko-rah-sohn)
diamond	diamante	(dee-uh-mon-teh)
pentagon	pentágono	(pen-tah-go-no)

Aprendamos las formas—
Let's Learn Shapes

Practice writing the Spanish words for these shapes.
Color the shapes.

línea

_____

cruz

_____

hexágono

_____

estrella

_____

Pronounce the shapes aloud.

line	línea	(lee-neh-uh)
cross	cruz	(kroos)
hexagon	hexágono	(hex-ah-go-no)
star	estrella	(es-tray-yuh)

Spanish Level 1—RBP0148

Busquemos las formas—
Searching for Shapes

Find and circle the words for shapes.

Can you find the formas (shapes)?

```
v n i o l u c r i c
z b p g e h y x c b
m g z v e s j v u o
h a h c e l f b b n
a c r u z n c e o o
d i a m a n t e r c
o l u g n a i r t a
r c u a d r a d o s
r z t l b y y g d t
a l l e r t s e l s
```

Word Bank

triángulo	cubo	cuadrado	cruz
diamante	esfera	estrella	cono
	flecha	círculo	

La cabeza y la cara—The Head and Face

Practice writing the Spanish words for parts of the head and face. Color the picture.

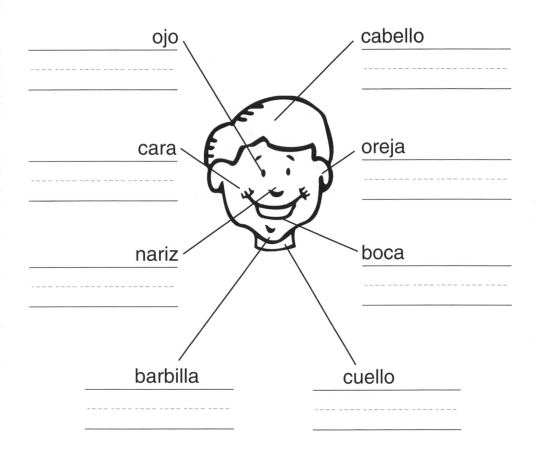

ojo

cabello

cara

oreja

nariz

boca

barbilla

cuello

La cabeza

Practice saying the words.

chin	barbilla	(bar-beh-yah)	face	cara	(kah-rah)
hair	cabello	(kah-bee-yoh)	ear	oreja	(oh-reh-ha)
eye	ojo	(oh-ho)	mouth	boca	(boh-cuh)
nose	nariz	(naw-rees)	neck	cuello	(kway-yoh)

El cuerpo—The Body

Write the Spanish names for the body in the spaces provided. Color the picture.

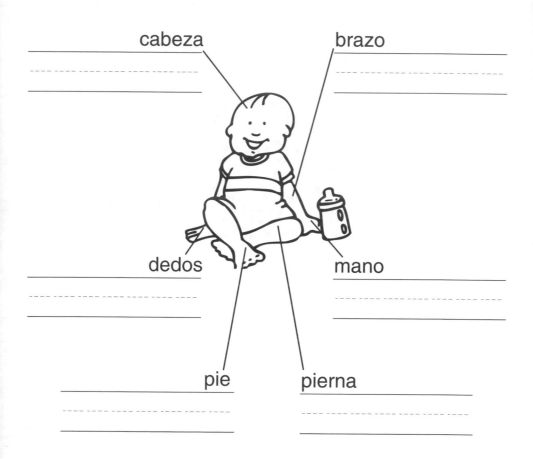

cabeza

brazo

dedos

mano

pie

pierna

El cuerpo

Practice saying the words.

head	cabeza	(kah-beh-suh)		arm	brazo	(brah-so)
hand	mano	(mah-no)		fingers	dedos	(deh-thos)
leg	pierna	(pee-air-nuh)		foot	pie	(pee-eh)

Emparejemos—Matching

Connect the name of the feature with its picture as shown. Then color the pictures.

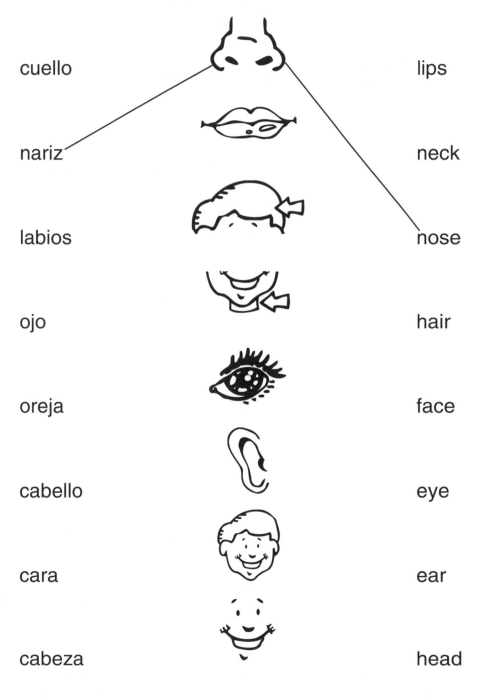

cuello

nariz

labios

ojo

oreja

cabello

cara

cabeza

lips

neck

nose

hair

face

eye

ear

head

Spanish Level 1—RBP0148

El cuerpo—The Body

Circle the correct word for the body part shown.

	(brazo)	bueno	bien
	pollo	pulmón	pierna
	corazón	cabeza	cuello
	diez	dedo	dueño
	menos	mano	más
	pie	dedo	por favor
	esfera	estilo	estómago

Sumas sencillas—Simple Sums

Write the correct numbers in the boxes as shown.

□	+	□	=	□
tres	más	tres	son	seis

□	+	□	=	□
dos	más	dos	son	cuatro

□	+	□	=	□
nueve	más	uno	son	diez

□	+	□	=	□
tres	más	cuatro	son	siete

□	+	□	=	□
ocho	más	dos	son	diez

□	–	□	=	□
diez	menos	ocho	son	dos

□	–	□	=	□
nueve	menos	seis	son	tres

□	–	□	=	□
ocho	menos	cuatro	son	cuatro

□	–	□	=	□
siete	menos	cuatro	son	tres

□	–	□	=	□
seis	menos	uno	son	cinco

Sumas sencillas—Simple Sums

Write the correct number in the boxes as shown.

[5]	+	[4]	=	[9]
cinco	más	cuatro	son	nueve

[ ]	+	[ ]	=	[ ]
ocho	más	dos	son	diez

[ ]	+	[ ]	=	[ ]
cuatro	más	tres	son	siete

[ ]	+	[ ]	=	[ ]
dos	más	siete	son	nueve

[ ]	+	[ ]	=	[ ]
uno	más	dos	son	tres

[ ]	–	[ ]	=	[ ]
seis	menos	uno	son	cinco

[ ]	–	[ ]	=	[ ]
cinco	menos	cuatro	son	uno

[ ]	–	[ ]	=	[ ]
ocho	menos	seis	son	dos

[ ]	–	[ ]	=	[ ]
nueve	menos	siete	son	dos

[ ]	–	[ ]	=	[ ]
diez	menos	nueve	son	uno

Busquemos los colores—
Searching for Colors
Find and circle the colors.

```
a  n  a  r  a  n  j  a  d  o
r  o  x  k  r  g  f  h  o  b
g  c  m  g  r  i  s  j  l  s
a  n  m  o  r  a  d  o  l  l
t  a  e  m  o  j  o  r  i  f
e  l  c  n  e  g  r  o  r  g
l  b  l  a  j  w  o  q  a  o
o  e  u  p  f  n  s  a  m  j
i  v  z  t  b  e  a  o  a  s
v  m  a  v  e  r  d  e  o  q
```

My favorite color is morado (purple).

Word Bank

morado	negro	blanco	amarillo
verde	rojo	rosa	gris
azul	café	anaranjado	violeta

Repasemos los colores—
Let's Review the Colors
Color in the picture with the color indicated in Spanish.

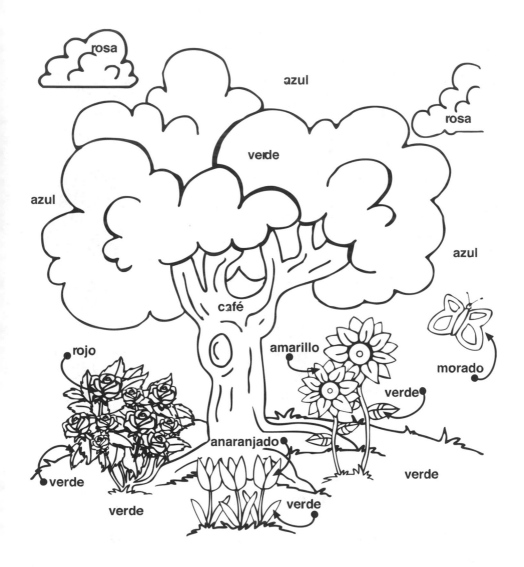

rosa

azul

rosa

verde

azul

azul

café

rojo

amarillo

morado

verde

anaranjado

verde

verde

verde

verde

¿De qué color es?— What Color Is It?

Write the correct color on the lines under each picture. Color the pictures.

café

Usa tu memoria—
Use Your Memory
Draw and color the correct shape.

corazón	estrella
triángulo	diamante
espiral	rectángulo
óvalo	círculo

Usa tu memoria— Use Your Memory

Draw and color the correct body feature.

ojo	nariz
mano	cabeza
oreja	cabello
pie	labios

La cabeza y la cara—
The Head and Face
Write the Spanish names for the
head and face in the spacesprovided.

Word Bank

ojo	cabeza	cabello
nariz	oreja	cara
cuello		boca

Página de respuestas—Answer Pages

Page 1
1. uno   **2.** dos   **3.** tres   **4.** cuatro
5. cinco

Page 2
6. seis   **7.** siete   **8.** ocho   **9.** nueve
10. diez

Page 3
seven—siete—7   three—tres—3
eight—ocho—8   two—dos—2
ten—diez—10   one—uno—1
four—cuatro—4   nine—nueve—9
five—cinco—5   six—seis—6

Page 4
5—cinco 10—diez 1—uno   7—siete
3—tres   6—seis

Page 5
siete   cuatro   seis   dos
diez   uno   ocho

Page 6
dos—2 rectangles colored
nueve—9 rectangles colored
cuatro—4 rectangles colored
uno—1 rectangle colored
ocho—8 rectangles colored
siete—7 rectangles colored
tres—3 rectangles colored
cinco—5 rectangles colored
diez—10 rectangles colored
seis—6 rectangles colored

Page 7
Aa, Bb, Cc, Ch ch, Dd

Page 8
Ee, Ff, Gg, Hh, Ii

Page 9
Jj, Kk, Ll, Ll ll, Mm, Nn

Page 10
Ññ, Oo, Pp, Qq, Rr

Page 11
Rr, rr, Ss, Tt, Uu, Vv

Page 12
Xx, Yy, Zz

Page 13
Practicing Spanish vowels

Pages 14–35
Practicing and reviewing the Spanish alphabet

Page 36
10. diez   **9.** nueve **8.** ocho   **7.** siete
6. seis   **5.** cinco **4.** cuatro **3.** tres
2. dos   **1.** uno

Page 37
11   once   12   doce
13   trece   14   catorce
15   quince   16   dieciséis
17   diecisiete   18   dieciocho
19   diecinueve   20   veinte

Page 38
seventeen—diecisiete—17
thirteen—trece—13
eighteen—dieciocho—18
twelve—doce—12
twenty—veinte—20
eleven—once—11
fourteen—catorce—14
nineteen—diecinueve—19
fifteen—quince—15
sixteen—dieciséis—16

Page 39
diecinueve   trece
veinte   dieciocho
dieciséis   catorce
doce

Page 39
diecinueve   trece
veinte   dieciocho
dieciséis   catorce
doce

Page 40
Writing practice

Página de respuestas—Answer Pages

Page 41–43
Learning colors

Page 44

- Red
- Orange
- Yellow
- Green
- Blue
- Purple

Page 45

negro	blanco	amarillo
café	rojo	azul

Page 46

anaranjado	morado	verde
violeta	rosa	gris

Page 47

azul—pond—blue
verde—frog—green
rojo—apple—red
amarillo—sun—yellow
gris—rain cloud—gray
blanco—snowflake—white
morado—grapes—purple
anaranjado—carrot—orange

Pages 48–57
Reviewing colors

Page 58

triángulo   cuadrado

círculo   rectángulo

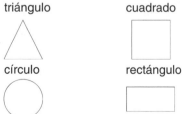

Page 59

cubo   cilindro

esfera   cono

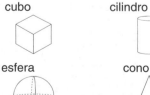

Page 60

flecha   corazón

diamante   pentágono

Page 61

línea   cruz

hexágono   estrella

Page 62

Page 63
Learning Spanish words for parts of the head and face

Page 64
Learning Spanish names for the body

Página de respuestas—Answer Pages

Page 65

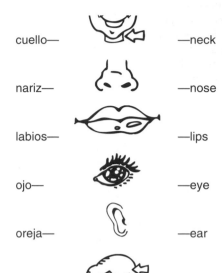

cuello—   —neck

nariz—   —nose

labios—   —lips

ojo—   —eye

oreja—   —ear

cabello—   —hair

cara—   —face

cabeza—   —head

Page 66

brazo	pierna
cabeza	dedo
mano	pie
estómago	

Page 67

$3 + 3 = 6$
$2 + 2 = 4$
$9 + 1 = 10$
$3 + 4 = 7$
$8 + 2 = 10$
$10 - 8 = 2$
$9 - 6 = 3$
$8 - 4 = 4$
$7 - 4 = 3$
$6 - 1 = 5$

Page 68

$5 + 4 = 9$
$8 + 2 = 10$
$4 + 3 = 7$
$2 + 7 = 9$
$1 + 2 = 3$
$6 - 1 = 5$
$5 - 4 = 1$
$8 - 6 = 2$
$9 - 7 = 2$
$10 - 9 = 1$

Page 69

Page 70

Página de respuestas—Answer Pages

Page 71

café

anaranjado

azul

rojo

verde

morado

Page 72

corazón

estrella

triángulo

diamante

espiral

rectángulo

óvalo

círculo

Page 73

ojo

nariz

mano

cabeza

oreja

cabello

pie

labios

Page 74

eye—ojo

face—cara

neck—cuello

mouth—boca

nose—nariz

ear—oreja

hair—cabello